BABY LOVE
Knitted Booties
for Tiny Feet

CATHERINE BOUQUEREL

sixth&springbooks
NEW YORK

For my three grandsons: Louis, Gaspard, and Thomas

Thank you to little Martin who had so much fun playing with his feet! Thanks to Sonia and Fabrice for styling the bootie photos so beautifully, and to all the team at Le Temps Apprivoisé. Thanks to Bergère de France for the stitch diagrams and for the yarns.

 **sixth&springbooks**

161 Avenue of the Americas
New York, New York 10013
sixthandspringbooks.com

FOR SIXTH&SPRING BOOKS

Editorial Director
JOY AQUILINO

Senior Editor
MICHELLE BREDESON

Art Director
DIANE LAMPHRON

Yarn Editor
RENÉE LORION

Associate Editor
ALEXANDRA JOINNIDES

Vice President, Publisher
TRISHA MALCOLM

Creative Director
JOE VIOR

Production Manager
DAVID JOINNIDES

President
ART JOINNIDES

FOR LTA

Editorial Director
VALÉRIE GENDREAU

Editor
ISABELLE REINER

Proofreader
NICOLE DEMEULENAERE

Graphic Design
ANNE BÉNOLIEL-DEFRÉVILLE

Layout
BÉNÉDICTE CHANTALOU / YURUGA

Photography
FABRICE BESSE

Stylist
SONIA ROY

Library of Congress Control Number: 2012931227

ISBN: 978-1-936096-38-1

Translation by Rosemary Perkins

1 3 5 7 9 10 8 6 4 2

First English Edition

PRINTED IN CHINA

Preface

What's more adorable than a baby's chubby little feet? What's more fun than making adorable booties to dress them?

Today's babies are fashionably dressed from day one after their mothers and grandmothers have spent the months leading up to their births knitting little outfits and booties to match.
I'm offering a few ideas that you can make as arrival gifts for newborns. Mommies will keep them as precious keepsakes of this tender time.

I took a great deal of pleasure in designing and making these little patterns. I hope you'll have as much fun knitting them.
If you're a beginner, take a few minutes to read the instructions and follow the sketches; you'll find them helpful for completing the patterns with ease.

Yours with lots of patience and a love for yarn!

Contents

Materials

- **Yarns** You'll use yarns in a variety of weights and fibers, including wool, wool blends, cotton, and acrylic. If you want to substitute yarns, find one with the same yarn weight number.

- **Knitting needles** The booties in this book were knitted with needles in the following sizes: size 2 (2.75mm), size 3 (3.25mm), size 4 (3.5mm), size 7 (4.5mm), and size 8 (5mm).

- **Crochet hook** A size B1 (2.25mm) crochet hook was used for several projects.

- **Trimmings** The right trimming adds an elegant, unique touch to your booties; try ribbons, beads, and fancy buttons.

Knitting basics

CASTING ON

1. Allowing a good length of yarn (about 3 times the intended width), form a slipknot and insert a needle through the central loop.
2. Wind the yarn loose end of the yarn around your left thumb, keeping the needle in your right hand.
3. Insert the needle under the loop around your left thumb; using your left hand, flip the yarn (that's coming from the ball) over the tip of the needle and pull the yarn toward you.
4. Pass the loop over the tip of the needle.
5. Gently pull the yarn on the left downwards: you've formed a stitch on the needle.
6. Repeat from step 2 until you have the number of stitches required to cast on for the pattern.

> **TIP**
>
> *For a neat edge, keep an even tension and always pull the yarn in the same direction. The stitches should slide easily on the needles without being too loose.*

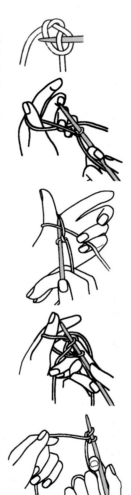

KNIT STITCH

Keep the yarn at the back of the work.

1. Insert the right-hand needle through the stitch from left to right, passing under the left-hand needle.
2. Pass the yarn over the right-hand needle from bottom to top.
3. Draw the right-hand needle with the loop slightly downward then back through the stitch.
4. Slip the old stitch off the left-hand needle: the new stitch is now on the right-hand needle.
5. Repeat steps 1–4 for each stitch. At the end of the row, all the stitches will be on the right-hand needle.

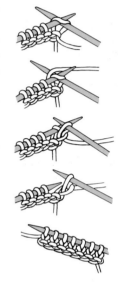

PURL STITCH

Keep the yarn in front of the work.

1. Insert the right-hand needle through the first stitch from right to left, passing under the left-hand needle.
2. Pass the yarn over the right-hand needle.
3. Draw the right-hand needle back through the stitch, pulling slightly to the right.
4. Slip the old stitch off the left-hand needle; the new stitch is now on the right-hand needle.
5. Repeat steps 1–4 for each stitch. At the end of the row, all the stitches will be on the right-hand needle.

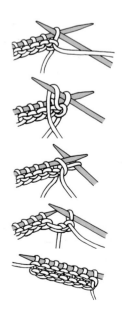

STOCKINETTE STITCH

Row 1 Knit (each stitch forms a V).
Row 2 Purl (each stitch forms a little horizontal "bar").
Repeat these 2 rows.

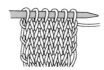

REVERSE STOCKINETTE STITCH

Row 1 Purl (each stitch forms a little horizontal "bar").
Row 2 Knit (each stitch forms a V).
Repeat these 2 rows.

GARTER STITCH

Knit every row.

K1, P1 RIB

Over an odd number of stitches:
Row 1 *K1, p1, repeat from * to end of row, ending with k1.
Row 2 *P1, k1, repeat from * to end of row, ending with p1.
Rep row 2 for k1, p1 rib.

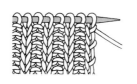

K2, P2 RIB

Over a multiple of 4 stitches plus 2:
Row 1 *K2, p2, repeat from * to end of row.
Row 2 Knit the knit stitches, purl the purl stitches.
Rep row 2 for k2, p2 rib.

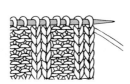

SEED STITCH

Over an odd number of stitches:
Row 1 *K1, p1, repeat from *, ending with k1.
Rep row 1 for seed st.

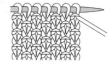

KNIT 2 TOGETHER (K2TOG)

Insert the right-hand needle into the next 2 stitches. Pass the yarn over the right-hand needle, draw the loop through both stitches, and slip both stitches off the left-hand needle. You now have 1 less stitch in the row.

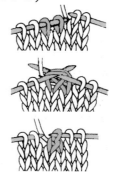

SLIPPED STITCH

Slip a stitch from the left-hand needle onto the right-hand needle without working it.

DOUBLE DECREASE (S2KP)

Slip the first 2 stitches as if to knit, knit the next st. Using the left-hand needle, pick up the 2 slipped stitches and pass them over the stitch you just worked. You now have 2 fewer stitches in the row.

YARN OVER (YO)

1. Between 2 stitches, pass the yarn over the right-hand needle to form a hole.
2. Continue according to the instructions to the end of the row.
3. In the next row, work the yarn-over loop as for the other stitches. You now have 1 extra stitch in the row.

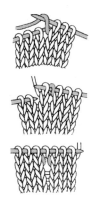

SINGLE DECREASE (SKP)

1. Slip a stitch, as if to knit from the left-hand needle to the right-hand needle; knit the next stitch.
2. Using the left-hand needle, pick up the slipped stitch and pass it over the stitch just worked.
3. You now have 1 less stitch in the row.

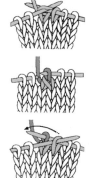

DOUBLE DECREASE (SK2P)

1. Slip a stitch, as if to knit from the left-hand needle to the right-hand needle; knit the next 2 stitches together.
2. Using the left-hand needle, pick up the slipped stitch and pass it over the 2 stitches just worked.
3. You now have 2 fewer stitches in the row.

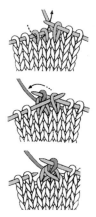

CARTRIDGE STITCH

Row 1 (RS) Purl.
Row 2 (WS) Knit.
Row 3 (RS) Knit.
Row 4 (WS) Purl.
Repeat these 4 rows.

ADDING STITCHES AT ENDS OF ROWS

Form loops by winding the yarn around the needle as many times as you need new stitches.
Work the new stitches according to the instructions.

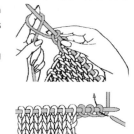

INCREASING 1 OR 2 STITCHES AT THE EDGES

At start of row, * knit 1 or 2, insert tip of right-hand needle under loop between 2 stitches (work through back of loop in order to twist the new st), knit the loop *.
At end of row, when 1 or 2 stitches remain, repeat from * to *, then knit to end.

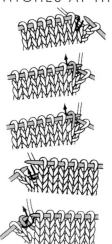

DECREASING 1 OR 2 STITCHES FROM THE EDGES

At start of row, knit 1 or 2, work a single decrease as above (SKP).
At end of row, when 1 or 2 stitches remain, knit 2 together, then knit to end.

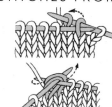

BINDING OFF

To form armholes or necks, or to finish off the work, bind off from left to right.

1. With right side facing, knit 2, pass the first st over the second and off the needles, then knit 1, pass the previous st over the one just worked and off the needles, and so on until you have bound off the number of stitches indicated.

2. With wrong side facing, work as for right side, but purl instead of knit.

ROUND BUTTONHOLES

This method is ideal for little round buttonholes.

When you have worked the number of stitches indicated, yarn over, knit 2 together, continue to end.

Next row Work the yarn-over loop as for the other stitches; the little hole will let the button through.

4-ST RIGHT (BACK) CABLE (4-ST RC)

Slip the next 2 stitches on to a cable needle, hold to back. Knit 2, then knit the 2 stitches from the cable needle.

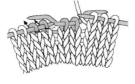

PICKING UP AND KNITTING STITCHES

Working in the direction of the knitting: With yarn at back and right side of work facing, * insert the needle through a stitch in the last row, pass the yarn over the needle

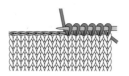

as if to knit, draw the loop through the stitch, and repeat from *.

- **At edge of knitting (ends of rows):**
  With yarn at back and right side of work facing, * insert the needle between the last 2 stitches, pass the yarn over the needle as if to knit, draw the loop through the

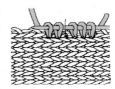

space between stitches, and repeat from * in 3 stitches all told, 1 in each of in 3 consecutive rows, then skip 1 row and repeat from *.

DUPLICATE STITCH

This method lets you work a small pattern on the right side of the work without having trails of yarn on the wrong side. Work the stitch from right to left. Using a blunt-tip (tapestry) needle, bring the yarn through from back to front at the base of a stitch, pass the needle under both strands of the stitch above, again insert the needle at

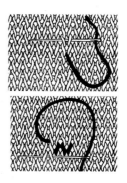

the base of the stitch and draw the yarn to the back of the work. You have worked 1 duplicate stitch.

INVISIBLE SEAMS

Work invisible seams with right side facing, between 2 sections knitted in the same direction, and using a tapestry needle and the same yarn as you used for the sections you're joining. Pass the yarn under

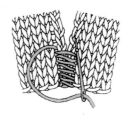

the horizontal strand between the 1st and 2nd stitches at the edge of a section, then under the matching strand of the other sections, pull firmly to make both sections meet, and continue to end. The seam will be invisible.

11

Hints and tips

> **IMPORTANT**
> *Even if your yarn is a little thicker than recommended, it's best to work with smaller needles to give firm body to the booties.*

STARTING A BALL OF YARN

Pull on the end of yarn that's tucked inside, so the yarn unwinds neatly without raveling.

FOR AN EVEN FABRIC

If you're a beginner, it's a good idea to practice on a few small, straight projects, such as a dolls' scarf or a coverlet for a bassinet. Make sure that the yarn is neither too taut nor too loose, so that the stitches slip easily over the needles.

FOR A NEAT EDGE

Always pull the first stitch of a row a little tighter; this will keep the work from stretching.

JOINING A NEW BALL OF YARN

Join a new ball at the beginning of a row. If you come across a join in the middle of a row, unpick to the beginning, cut the yarn at the knot, and work the row again.

TO PICK UP A DROPPED STITCH

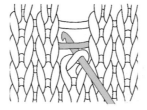

Pass a crochet hook through the dropped stitch, then hook the horizontal strand just above the dropped stitch and pass it through.Repeat for as many rows as you need, and slip the final loop on to the left-hand needle.

ABBREVIATIONS

Using abbreviations makes it faster and easier to follow the instructions.

beg	beginning
4-st RC	4-stitch right (back) cable
ch st	chain stitch
cont	continue
dec	decrease
dc	double crochet
SK2P or S2KP	double decrease
dpn(s)	double-pointed needle(s)
foll	following/follows
inc	increase
k	knit
k2tog	knit 2 stitches together
lp(s)	loop(s)
p	purl
rep	repeat
rev	reverse
rnd	round
r	row(s)
RS	right side
sc	single crochet
SKP	single decrease
sl	slip
sl st	slip stitch
st(s)	stitch(es)
Stst.	stockinette stitch
tog	together
WS	wrong side
yo	yarn over

Crochet basics

CHAIN STITCH (BASE CHAIN)

Form a slipknot and pass the crochet hook through the central loop. * Pass the yarn over the hook (yarn over), draw the yarn through the loop on the hook: you have just worked a stitch. Rep from * until you have worked as many chain stitches as indicated.

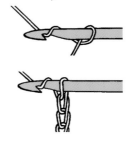

13

> **BOBBLES**
> *To make a small bobble, work 3 chain stitches, * yo, insert hook into the 1st of the 3 chain stitches, draw up loop, yarn over and through first 2 loops on hook*, rep from * to * 3 times. Close by working yarn over and through all 5 remaining loops on hook.*

SLIP STITCH

Insert the hook into a stitch, yarn over, draw loop up and through the stitch on the hook.

SINGLE CROCHET

Insert the hook into a stitch, * yarn over, draw up loop, repeat from * and draw loop through both loops on the hook.

DOUBLE CROCHET

Yarn over, insert the hook into a stitch, yarn over, draw up loop, yarn over and through first 2 loops on hook, yarn over and through 2 loops on hook.

my blossom   my love-bug   my sweetheart   my precious

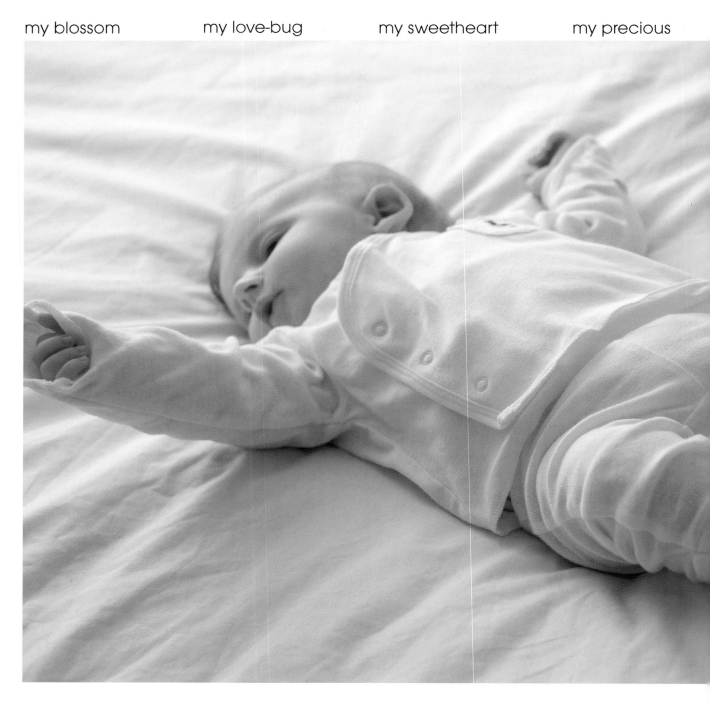

"How many ways do I love you?
How many times can you tap your shoe?

my lamb   my sweetie-pie   my cherub

my darling

my chickadee

my love

my angel-face

my baby

I'll tell you how your mommy's love grows,
With warm little socks for your precious toes."

Special day

Time for a beautiful ceremony. The big day is here!

BOOTIE

SIZES
Newborn to 3 months
(3 to 6 months)

MATERIALS
• *1 1¾oz/50g ball*
(approx 191yd/175m) of
Bernat Baby (acrylic/
nylon) in 35402 White ▣
• *2 pairs size 3 (3.25mm)*
needles
• *2 satin ribbon bows*

STITCHES
stockinette stitch
reverse stockinette stitch
garter stitch
cartridge stitch
k2tog
SKP
SK2P
fancy pattern st

GAUGE
28 sts to 4"/10cm over St
st using size 3 (3.25mm)
needles.
Take time to check
gauge.

Beg at the ankle.

Using size 3 (3.25mm) needles cast on 43 sts (both sizes) and work in garter st for 4 rows, then in stockinette st for 2 rows.

Next row Beg fancy pattern st by working the foll 2 rows 4 times:

Row 1 (RS) K1, SKP, * k2, yo, k1, yo, k2, SK2P *, rep from * to * 3 times; end by working k2, yo, k1, yo, k2, k2tog, k1.

Row 2 (WS) Knit (reverse stockinette st).

Next row Cont in stockinette st *decreasing for smaller size only* 4 times evenly over the course of the row—37 (50) sts.

Next row Leave 13 (18) sts on a spare needle, work the next 11 (14) sts and turn; leave the remaining 13 (18) sts on a spare needle and cont over the central 11 (14) sts in stockinette st for 10 (12) rows.

Next row Work across the 13 (18) sts from the first spare needle, pick up and knit 9 (11) sts on the right side, work across the 11 (14) central sts, pick up and knit 9 (11) sts on the left side, then work across the remaining 13 (18) sts from the second spare needle—57 (65) sts.

Cont in cartridge st (see p. 10) for 14 rows.

Next row Leave the first 23 (25) sts on a spare needle; work across the next 11 (14) sts for the sole, turn the work.

Next row K 10 (13), then knit tog the last st of the sole with the first of the sts left aside. Cont in garter st, ending each row by knitting tog the last st of the sole with the first of the sts left aside, until 5 (7) sts remain at each side of bootie. Bind off.

Sew up the heel seam and slipstitch a bow to the front of the bootie. Complete a second, identical bootie.

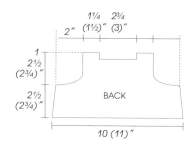

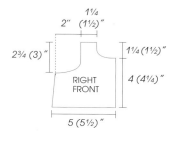

LITTLE VEST

BACK

Using size 3 (3.25mm) needles cast on 67 (75) sts and work in garter st for 4 rows, followed by stockinette st for 2 rows.

Next row Beg fancy pattern st by working the foll 2 rows 4 times:

Row 1 (RS) K1, SKP, * k2, yo, k1, yo, k2, SK2P *, rep from * to * 3 times; end by working k2, yo, k1, yo, k2, k2tog, k1. **Row 2 (WS)** Knit (reverse stockinette st).

Next row Switch to stockinette st and dec 9 (10) times evenly over the course of the row—58 (65) sts.

Cont straight in stockinette st until back measures 2½ (3)"/6 (8)cm from cast-on edge, then shape armholes as follows: Bind off 4 sts at beg of next 2 rows, 3 sts at beg of foll 2 rows, then 1 st at beg of foll 4 rows—36 (43) sts. Cont straight until back measures 3 (3½)"/8 (9)cm from cast-on edge, then switch to cartridge st (see p. 10) and work straight until back measures 5 (6)"/13 (15)cm from cast-on edge.

Next row Work 8 (10) sts in cartridge st and place these sts on a stitch holder; complete the 2 sides separately from this point. Bind off the next 20 (23) sts for the neck and work to end. Work 2 rows even.

Next row With WS facing, bind off the remaining 8 (10) sts for the shoulder. With WS facing, work across the sts on the holder and complete the right back to match.

RIGHT FRONT

Using size 3 (3.25mm) needles cast on 35 (43) sts and work in fancy pattern st from * to * as given for the back 3 (4) times.

Next row Switch to stockinette st and dec 5 (6) times evenly over the course of the row—30 (37) sts. Cont straight until right front measures 2½ (3)"/6 (8)cm from cast-on edge, then shape the armhole as follows: Bind off 4 sts at beg of next WS row, 3 sts at beg of foll WS row, 2 sts at beg of next WS row, and 1 st at beg of foll WS row twice—19 (26) sts. Cont straight until right front measures 3 (3½)"/8 (9)cm from cast-on edge.

Next row Switch to cartridge st and cont straight until right front measures 4 (4¾)"/10 (12)cm from cast-on edge, then shape neck by binding off at beg of RS rows as follows: 6 sts once, 2 (3) sts once, 1 (2) sts 3 (2) times, 0 (1) st 0 (3) times—8 (10) sts. Cont straight until right front measures 5½ (6)"/13.5 (15.5)cm from cast-on edge, ending with an RS row.

Next row With WS facing, bind off remaining sts for shoulder.

LEFT FRONT

Work as for right front, reversing the shaping.

FINISHING

Sew the shoulder seams. Using size 2 (2.75mm) needles, beg at right back underarm with RS facing, pick up and knit 48 (56) sts around the armhole. Work in garter st for 3 rows. Bind off. Rep for left armhole, beg at left front underarm with RS facing. Beg at right front with RS facing, pick up and knit 52 (60) sts around the neck. Work in garter st for 3 rows. Bind off. Beg at top left front with RS facing, pick up and knit 26 (34) sts down left front. Work in garter st for 3 rows. Bind off. Repeat for right front, beg at lower edge with RS facing. Sew the side seams. Attach the press stud to the right and left fronts; slip stitch the bow at center front.

Cross my heart

I'll be the prettiest girl on the dance floor . . .

SIZES
*Newborn to 3 months
(3 to 6 months)*

MATERIALS
• *1 1¾oz/50g ball (each approx 196yd/180m) of Bergère de France Caline (acrylic/wool/polyamide) in Porcinet (light pink)*
• *size 2 (2.75mm) needles*
• *4 pink heart-shaped buttons*

STITCHES
*garter stitch
seed stitch
SK2P*

GAUGE
*27 sts to 4"/10cm over St st using size 2 (2.5mm) needles.
Take time to check gauge.*

SOLE
Cast on 41 (45) sts and work 1 row in seed st. Now cont in seed st and inc every 2 rows as follows:

Next row K1, inc 1, work 19 (21) in pattern, inc 1, k1, inc 1, k19 (21), inc 1, k1.

Next row K2, inc 1, work 19 (21) in pattern, inc 1, k3, inc 1, k19 (21), inc 1, k2.

Next row K3, inc 1, work 19 (21) in pattern, inc 1, k5, inc 1, k19 (21), inc 1, k3.

Next row K4, inc 1, work 19 (21) in pattern, inc 1, k7, inc 1, k19 (21), inc 1, k4—55 (61) sts.

Cont straight in seed st for 10 rows, then dec every 2 rows as follows:

Next row Work 22 (24) in pattern, SK2P, work 5, SK2P, work 22 (24).

Next row Work 21 (23) in pattern, SK2P, k3, SK2P, work 21 (23).

Next row Work 20 (22) in pattern, * SK2P *, rep from * to * twice, work 20 (22)—43 (47) sts.

STRAPS
Next row *K10 (12), turn *, rep from * to *, then k10 (12) and cast on another 20 sts—30 (32) sts.

Next row Bind off the 30 (32) sts knitwise.

Pick up the remaining sts, bind off 23 sts, cast on 20 sts using the free needle, then work across the remaining 10 (12) sts—30 (32) sts. Complete 3 rows in garter st. Loosely bind off knitwise.

FINISHING
Sew the sole and the back of the bootie.
Cross the straps over the instep and hold in place by attaching a button at the end of each strap.
Complete a second, identical bootie.

My first espadrilles

So light and irresistible for my pretty feet!

SIZES
Newborn to 3 months (3 to 6 months)

MATERIALS
• *1 1¾oz/50g ball (approx 131yd/120m) of Rowan/Westminster Fibers Organic Cotton Naturally Dyed DK in 986 Natural*
• *Small amount of blue cotton yarn for embroidery*
• *size 4 (3.5mm) needles*
• *size B/1 (2.25mm)*
• *crochet hook*

STITCHES
garter stitch
stockinette stitch
SK2P
k2tog, k3tog
crochet chain stitch
straight stitch

GAUGE
24 sts to 4"/10cm over St st using size 4 (3.5mm) needles.
Take time to check gauge.

SOLE
Using the size 4 (3.5mm) needles, cast on 35 (39) sts and knit 1 row. Continuing in garter st, inc every 2 rows as follows:

Next row K1, inc 1, k16 (18), inc 1, k1, inc 1, k16 (18), inc 1, k1.

Next row K2, inc 1, k16 (18), inc 1, k3, inc 1, k16 (18), inc 1, k2.

Next row K3, inc 1, k16 (18), inc 1, k5, inc 1, k16 (18), inc 1, k3.

Next row K4, inc 1, k16 (18), inc 1, k7, inc 1, k16 (18), inc 1, k4—51 (55) sts.

Cont in garter st for 10 rows. Bind off.

UPPER
Cast on 12 (14) sts and work in garter st for 4 rows.

Next row Switch to stockinette st and work straight for 5 (3) rows.

Next row With RS facing, sl 1, k1, psso, knit until 2 sts remain, k2tog.

Work 1 row straight.

Larger size only: Repeat the last 2 rows once.

Next row (row 6 (12)) Sl1, k2tog, k2, k3tog—6 sts remain.

Work 1 row straight.

Next row (row 8 (14)) Bind off remaining sts (toe).

FINISHING
Sew up the sole and back of the espadrille, followed by the upper. Using the crochet hook, work 100 ch sts for a tie and fasten off. Fold the tie in half and attach the fold at the top of the heel. Follow the design below to embroider the flower in straight stitch. Complete a second, identical espadrille.

22

Darling daisies

She loves me, she loves me not. . .

SIZES
Newborn to 3 months (3 to 6 months)

MATERIALS
• 1 1¾oz/50g ball (approx 137yd/140m) each of Debbie Bliss/KFI Eco Baby (organic cotton) in #20 Mint and #14 Banana
• 2 daisy-shaped buttons
• size 2 (2.75mm) needles
• 2 press studs

STITCHES
garter stitch
stockinette stitch
single dec (SK2P)
p2tog

GAUGE
26 sts to 4"/10cm over St st using size 2 (2.75mm) needles.
Take time to check gauge.

SOLE
Using Banana, cast on 33 (37) sts and knit 1 row, then cont in garter st and inc as follows:
Next row K2, inc 1, k14 (16), inc 1, k1, inc 1, k14 (16), inc 1, k2. Work 1 row straight.
Next row K3, inc 1, k14 (16), inc 1, k3, inc 1, k14 (16), inc 1, k3. Work 1 row straight.
Next row K4, inc 1, k14 (16), inc 1, k5, inc 1, k14 (16), inc 1, k4. Work 1 row straight.
Next row K5, inc 1, k14 (16), inc 1, k7, inc 1, k14 (16), inc 1, k5—49 (53) sts.
Work 2 rows straight in garter st. Do not cut yarn.

EDGE OF SOLE
Join in Mint yarn and work in stockinette st for 7 rows.
Next row With WS facing, p2tog the 1st st on the needle with the same st 7 rows down. Continue working 2 sts tog in this way to end of row. Now switch to garter st and knit 2 rows Banana followed by 4 rows Mint, then dec as follows:
Next row K18 (20), SKP, k9, k2tog, k18 (20).
Next row K18 (20), SKP, k7, k2tog, k18 (20).
Next row K18 (20), SKP, k5, k2tog, k18 (20).
Next row K18 (20), SKP, k3, k2tog, k18 (20).
Next row K18 (20), SKP, k1, k2tog, k18 (20)—39 (43) sts.
Next row K10 (12) sts and place them on a spare needle; bind off the next 8 sts; * k3, turn the work, rep from * 7 times to form the strap slot; bind off the 3 sts just worked and

cut the yarn. Rejoin yarn and bind off the next 8 sts; knit to end, then cast on 22 sts to form the ankle strap. Work 4 rows in garter st across all sts, then bind off loosely. Complete the second bootie, reversing the shaping for the ankle strap.

FINISHING
Sew the sole and back seams. Fold the strap slot in half and slip stitch to the inside; thread the ankle strap through it. Sew a press stud onto the inside of each strap and the outside of the bootie, and attach a button to the outside of the strap.

Mix and match

Why do my feet look different?

TRICOLOR BOOTIE
SOLE
Using Mauve, cast on 40 (44) sts, work 1 row in stockinette st, and cont in stockinette st, inc as follows:

Next row K2, inc 1, k16 (18), inc 1, k4, inc 1, k16 (18), inc 1, k2. Work 1 row straight.

Next row K3, inc 1, k16 (18), inc 1, k6, inc 1, k16 (18), inc 1, k3. Work 1 row straight.

Next row K4, inc 1, k16 (18), inc 1, k8, inc 1, k16 (18), inc 1, k4. Work 1 row straight.

Next row K5, inc 1, k16 (18), inc 1, k10, inc 1, k16 (18), inc 1, k5—56 (60) sts.

Cont straight in reverse stockinette st for 3 rows then, on the next row, switch to stockinette stitch and change yarns as follows, twisting yarn loosely at back of work to avoid forming holes: K28 (30) Teal, k28 (30) Pea Green. Work straight in 2 colors for 8 rows, then beg with row 9, dec as follows:

Next row K24 (26), * SKP, rep from *, ** k2tog, rep from **, k24 (26). Work 1 row straight.

Next row K22 (24), * SKP, rep from *, ** k2tog, rep from **, k22 (24). Work 1 row straight.

Next row K20 (22), * SKP, rep from *, ** k2tog, rep from **, k20 (22). Work 1 row straight.

Next row K18 (20), * SKP, rep from *, ** k2tog, rep from **, k18 (20). Work 1 row straight.

Next row K16 (18), * SKP, rep from *, ** k2tog, rep from **, k16 (18)—36 (40) sts.

Next row Switch to Mauve and work in stockinette st for 8 rows. Bind off loosely.

STRIPED BOOTIE
Cast on and work as for tricolor bootie, working the edge of the sole in Teal and following the instructions for striped stockinette stitch.

FINISHING
Sew the sole and back seams, then attach one button at center front of each bootie.

At the beach

I'm going to the beach to build a giant sand castle . . .

SIZES

Newborn to 3 months (3 to 6 months)

MATERIALS

- *1 1¾oz/50g ball (approx 137yd/140m) each of Debbie Bliss/KFI Eco Baby (organic cotton) in #6 Pea Green, #5 Teal, #23 Light Peach, #24 Apricot, #22 Pinkish Burgundy, and #12 Bubble Gum* 🄰
- *size 2 (2.75mm) needles*
- *2 pink buttons*

STITCHES

garter stitch
yarn over
k2tog

GAUGE

26 sts to 4"/10cm over St st using size 2 (2.75mm) needles.
Take time to check gauge.

SOLE

Using Pinkish Burgundy for the left foot and Apricot for the right, cast on 38 (42) sts and knit 1 row, then cont in garter st, increasing as follows:

Next row K2, inc 1, k16 (18), inc 1, k2, inc 1, k16 (18), inc 1, k2. Work 1 row straight.

Next row K3, inc 1, k16 (18), inc 1, k4, inc 1, k16 (18), inc 1, k3. Work 1 row straight.

Next row K4, inc 1, k16 (18), inc 1, k6, inc 1, k16 (18), inc 1, k4. Work 1 row straight.

Next row K5, inc 1, k16 (18), inc 1, k8, inc 1, k16 (18), inc 1, k5—54 (58) sts.

Knit 2 rows straight. Bind off.

SMALL BAND

Using Pea Green for the left and Teal for the right, cast on 12 (14) sts and work in garter st for 4 rows. Bind off.

LARGE BAND

Using Bubble Gum for the left and Light Peach for the right, cast on 16 (18) sts and work in garter st for 4 rows. Bind off.

ANKLE STRAP

Use Teal for the left and Pea Green for the right, and work eyelet buttonholes at opposite ends of the straps.

Cast on 34 (36) sts and work in garter st for 4 rows, forming a buttonhole at beg (or end) of row 2 as follows: K2 (knit until 4 sts remain), yo, k2tog, knit to end. On completing row 4, bind off.

FINISHING

Slip stitch the small band in place near the end of the sole and sew the large band ¼"/0.5cm higher. Fold the ankle strap in thirds and sew the first fold to center back, allowing two-thirds to go around the ankle and placing the buttonhole at either left or right.

Junior sailor

Hoist the sails . . . I'm on deck with Daddy!

SIZES
*Newborn to 3 months
(3 to 6 months)*

MATERIALS
- *1 1¾oz/50g ball (each approx 103yd/95m) each of Bergère de France Bergerine (wool/cotton) in Etang (blue), Rotin (brown), and Pyramide (beige)*
- *size 6 (4mm) needles*
- *size B/1 (2.25mm) crochet hook*

STITCHES
*stockinette stitch
garter stitch
bobble
crochet chain stitch*

GAUGE
*21 sts to 4"/10cm over St st using size 6 (4mm) needles.
Take time to check gauge.*

SOLE
Begin at the heel: Using brown, cast on 9 (11) sts and work in garter st for 28 (32) rows. **Next row** Switch to blue, cast on 18 (20) sts, k9 (11), cast on 18 (20) sts—45 (51) sts. Cont in garter st for 10 rows.

UPPER
Next row With RS facing, k9 (10), bind off 9 (11), k9 (10), bind off 9 (10), k9 (10).
Next row With WS facing, place the first 9 (10) sts on a stitch holder. Join beige yarn and work in stockinette st over the central 9 (11) sts, turn the work; place the remaining 9 (10) sts on a stitch holder and cont in stockinette st over the central sts for a total of 10 rows. Bind off loosely. With WS facing, rejoin blue yarn to work across all the sts from the holders and cont in garter st for 12 rows all told. Bind off loosely.

FINISHING
Sew the upper and the sole to the sides of the bootie, then join the back seam. Using the crochet hook and beige yarn, work 80 (90) ch sts for "laces." Using brown, follow the instructions to crochet a bobble at each end of the lace. Fold the lace in half and attach the fold at center back, turn the cuff down over the lace; tie the lace in front. Make a second, identical bootie.

HAT

SIZES
*Newborn to 3 months
(3 to 6 months)*

MATERIALS
• *1 1¾oz/50g ball (each
approx 103yd/95m)
each of Bergère de
France Bergerine (wool/
cotton) in Etang (blue),
Rotin (brown), and
Pyramide (beige)* 🔳
• *size 6 (4mm) needles*
• *size B/1 (2.25mm)
crochet hook*

STITCHES
*stockinette stitch
garter stitch
k2tog
single dec (SKP)
crochet: chain stitch,
bobble*

GAUGE
*21 sts and 28 rows to
4"/10cm over St st using
size 6 (4mm) needles.
Take time to check
gauge.*

Using the size 4 (3.5mm) needles and brown, cast on 46 (50) sts and work in garter st for 12 rows. Leave the work on a spare needle. Again using the size 4 (3.5mm) needles and brown, cast on 28 (32) sts and work in garter st for 12 rows. Using the same needle, knit across all the sts left aside—74 (82) sts. Cont in garter st for 12 rows. Next row Switch to blue and work in stockinette st for 16 (20) rows, then switch to beige, cont straight in stockinette stitch for 2 rows, and shape the hat as follows:

Next row K8 (9), SKP, * k2tog, k14 (16), SKP *, rep from * to * twice, k2tog, k8 (9). Work 1 row straight.

Next row K7 (8), SKP, * k2tog, k12 (14), SKP *, rep from * to * twice, k2tog, k7 (8). Work 1 row straight.

Next row K6 (7), SKP, * k2tog, k10 (12), SKP *, rep from * to * twice, k2tog, k6 (7). Work 1 row straight.

Next row K5 (6), SKP, * k2tog, k8 (10), SKP *, rep from * to * twice, k2tog, k5 (6). Work 1 row straight.

Next row K4 (5), SKP, * k2tog, k6 (8), SKP *, rep from * to * twice, k2tog, k4 (5). Work 1 row straight.

Next row K3 (4), SKP, * k2tog, k4 (6), SKP *, rep from * to * twice, k2tog, k3 (4). Work 1 row straight.

Next row K2 (3), SKP, * k2tog, k2 (4), SKP *, rep from * to * twice, k2tog, k2 (3). Work 1 row straight.

Next row K1 (2), SKP, * k2tog, k0 (2), SKP *, rep from * to * twice, k2tog, k1 (2)—10 (18) sts. **Larger size only** Work 1 row straight.

Next row K1, SKP, * k2tog, SKP *, rep from * to * twice, k2tog, k1—10 sts.

Cut the yarn, leaving a length of about 10"/25cm. Pass the yarn through the remaining sts and pull firmly to close. Fasten off with a few stitches and sew up the seam. Using the crochet hook and beige, work 180 ch sts and work back over the base chain with 1 sc in each st. Fasten off. Using brown, work a bobble at each end of the cord. Tie the cord around the hat inside the brim, holding it in place with a few little stitches. Tie the cord as shown in the photo.

33

Fresh strawberries

I'm going to help Mommy make jam . . .

SIZES

Newborn to 3 months
(3 to 6 months)

MATERIALS

• 1 3oz/85g ball (approx
237yd/217m) each of
Bernat Satin Sport
(acrylic) in 03705 Rouge
and 03040 Black and
03225 Leap Frog
(green) ③
• elastic thread
• size 4 (3.5mm) needles

STITCHES

garter stitch
stockinette stitch
single dec (SKP)
SK2P
k2tog
k2, p2 rib
duplicate stitch

GAUGE

24 sts to 4"10cm over St
st using size 4 (3.5mm)
needles and Satin Sport.
Take time to check
gauge.

SOLE

Using Rouge, cast on 38 (42) sts and knit 1 row, then cont in garter st, increasing as follows:

Next row K2, inc 1, k16 (18), inc 1, k2, inc 1, k16 (18), inc 1, k2. Work 1 row straight.

Next row K3, inc 1, k16 (18), inc 1, k4, inc 1, k16 (18), inc 1, k3. Work 1 row straight.

Next row K4, inc 1, k16 (18), inc 1, k6, inc 1, k16 (18), inc 1, k4. Work 1 row straight.

Next row K5, inc 1, k16 (18), inc 1, k8, inc 1, k16 (18), inc 1, k5. Work 1 row straight.

Next row K6, inc 1, k16 (18), inc 1, k10, inc 1, k16 (18), inc 1, k6—58 (62) sts.

UPPER

Cont in garter st for 2 more rows. Switch to stockinette st and work 8 rows straight, then shape as follows:

Next row K24 (26), *SKP twice, k2, k2tog twice, k24 (26). Work 1 row straight.

Next row K22 (24), *SKP twice, k2, k2tog twice, K22 (24). Work 1 row straight.

Next row K20 (22), *SKP twice, k2, k2tog twice, k20 (22). Work 1 row straight.

Next row K18 (20), *SKP twice, k2, k2tog twice, k18 (20). Work 1 row straight.

Next row K16 (18), *SKP twice, k2, k2tog twice, k16 (18). Work 1 row straight—38 (42) sts.

Larger size only: Next row K16, *SKP twice, k2, k2tog twice, k18—38 sts.

CUFF

Using Green, work in k2, p2 rib for 5 rows, then beg the cuff on the WS, which will turn into the RS. **Next row** With WS facing, bind off 1 st, then work * k1, SKP, k3, k2tog, k1, turn the work, p7, turn the work, k1, SKP, k1, k2tog, k1, turn the work, p5, turn the work, k1, sl 1, k2tog, k1, turn the work, p3, turn the work, SK2P, cut the yarn and pass it through the remaining st *. Rep from * to * 4 times. Bind off the remaining st.

FINISHING

Sew the sole and back seams. Turn down the cuff and hold it in place with a few small stitches. Using Black, embroider the seeds in duplicate st (see chart) over staggered rows on both sides of the bootie.

For the black loop: Cast on 15 sts and knit 2 rows (garter st). Bind off. Fold the strip in half and sew the 2 ends tog at center back. Use the tapestry needle to pass the elastic thread through the first row of Green ribbing. Complete a second, identical bootie.

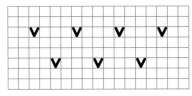

V duplicate st in black

Peter Pan

I'll fly away home with my lucky ladybug!

SIZES
*Newborn to 3 months
(3 to 6 months)*

MATERIALS
• 1 1¾oz/50g ball
(approx 126yd/115m) of
Rowan Cashsoft DK
(cashmere/merino wool/
acrylic microfiber) in 541
Spruce (dark green) 🄱
• 1.88oz/25g ball (approx
229yd/210m) of Rowan
Kidsilk Haze (super kid
mohair/silk) in 581
Meadow (light green) 🄰
• one pair each size 2
(2.75mm) and 4 (3.5mm)
needles
• 2 ladybug-shaped
buttons

STITCHES
*garter stitch
stockinette stitch
k2tog
yarn over
single dec (SKP)
SK2P*

GAUGE
*24 sts to 4"/10cm over St
st using size 4 (3.5mm)
needles using Cashsoft
DK.
Take time to check
gauge.*

SOLE
Using size 3 (3.25mm) needles and Dark Green, cast on 33 (37) sts and knit 1 row (garter st). Cont in garter st and inc as follows:
Next row K1, inc 1, k15 (17), inc 1, k1, inc 1, k15 (17), inc 1, k1. Work 1 row straight.
Next row K2, inc 1, k15 (17), inc 1, k3, inc 1, k15 (17), inc 1, k2. Work 1 row straight.
Next row K3, inc 1, k15 (17), inc 1, k5, inc 1, k15 (17), inc 1, k3. Work 1 row straight.
Next row K4, inc 1, k15 (17), inc 1, k7, inc 1, k15 (17), inc 1, k4. Work 1 row straight.
Next row K5, inc 1, k15 (17), inc 1, k9, inc 1, k15 (17), inc 1, k5—53 (57) sts.

UPPER
Cont in garter st for 2 rows, then in next row, switch to stockinette stitch and work straight for 8 rows, then shape upper as follows:
Next row K23 (25), SKP, SK2P, k2tog, k23 (25). Work 1 row straight.
Next row K21 (23), SKP, SK2P, k2tog, k21 (23). Work 1 row straight.
Next row K19 (21), SKP, SK2P, k2tog, k19 (21). Work 1 row straight.
Next row K17 (19), SKP, SK2P, k2tog, k17 (19). Cont straight in garter st for 4 rows, then in stockinette stitch for 4 rows. Bind off loosely.

LARGE LEAF
Using size 2 (2.75mm) needles and light green yarn, cast on 7 sts and work in stockinette st, shaping every 2 rows as follows, beg with next row:
Next row K3, yo, k1, yo, k3. Work 1 row straight.
Next row K4, yo, k1, yo, k4. Work 1 row straight.
Next row K5, yo, k1, yo, k5. Work 1 row straight.
Next row K6, yo, k1, yo, k6. Work 1 row straight.
Then, every 2 rows beg with next row:
Next row K1, k2tog, k9, SKP, k1. Work 1 row straight.

Next row K1, k2tog, k7, SKP, k1. Work 1 row straight.
Next row K1, k2tog, k5, SKP, k1. Work 1 row straight.
Next row K1, k2tog, k3, SKP, k1. Work 1 row straight.
Next row K1, k2tog, k1, SKP, k1. Work 1 row straight.
Next row K1, SKP, k1. Work 1 row straight.
Next row SK2P.

SMALL LEAF
Using size 2 (2.25mm) needles and Light Green yarn, cast on 5 sts and work in stockinette st, increasing every 2 rows (work 1 row straight after every inc row) as follows:
Next row K2, yo, k1, yo, k2.
Next row K3, yo, k1, yo, k3.
Next row K4, yo, k1, yo, k4.
Then work every 2 rows (working 1 row straight after every dec row) as follows:
Next row K1, k2tog, k5, SKP, k1.
Next row K1, k2tog, k3, SKP, k1.
Next row K1, k2tog, k1, SKP, k1.
Next row K1, SKP, k1.
Next row SK2P.

FINISHING
Sew the seams for the sole and the back, attach the small and large leaves to the ankle at center back, then sew the ladybug button on top of the leaves.

Ladybug

Let's count the spots. 1, 2, 3 . . . 6!

SIZES

*Newborn to 3 months
(3 to 6 months)*

MATERIALS

• *1 3oz/85g ball (approx
237yd/217m) each of
Bernat Satin Sport
(acrylic) in 03705 Rouge
and 03040 Black* (**3**)
• *size 4 (3.5mm) needles*
• *size B/1 (2.25mm)
crochet hook*

STITCHES

*garter stitch
k2tog
crochet chain stitch,
single crochet, slip stitch*

GAUGE

*24 sts to 4"/10cm over
St st using size 4 (3.5mm)
needles.
Take time to check
gauge.*

SOLE

Using Black, cast on 33 (37) sts and knit 1 row, then cont in garter st, increasing every 2 rows as follows:

Next row K1, inc 1, k15 (17), inc 1, k1, inc 1, k15 (17), inc 1, k1. Work 1 row straight.

Next row K2, inc 1, k15 (17), inc 1, k3, inc 1, k15 (17), inc 1, k2. Work 1 row straight.

Next row K3, inc 1, k15 (17), inc 1, k5, inc 1, k15 (17), inc 1, k3. Work 1 row straight.

Next row K4, inc 1, k15 (17), inc 1, k7, inc 1, k15 (17), inc 1, k4. Work 1 row straight.

Next row K5, inc 1, k15 (17), inc 1, k9, inc 1, k15 (17), inc 1, k5—53 (57) sts.

UPPER

Cont straight in garter st for 4 rows, then k21 (23) and place these sts on a stitch holder, k11, turn the work, and place the remaining 20 (23) sts on a stitch holder. Cont working over the central 11 sts, increasing as follows: *K1, inc 1, knit until 1 st remains, inc 1, k1 **. Work 1 row straight *. Rep from * to * twice and again from * to ** once—19 sts. Knit 4 rows straight. Bind off.

Using Rouge, with WS facing, work across the 21 (23) sts from the first holder and work 4 rows in garter st.

Next row With WS facing (toe edge of bootie), bind off 3 sts—17 (20) sts. Knit 16 rows straight.

Next row Switch to Black and knit 2 more rows. Bind off.

Using Rouge, with RS facing, work across the remaining 20 (23) sts and knit 4 rows all told.

Next row With RS facing (toe edge), bind off 3 sts—17 (20) sts. Knit 16 rows straight.

Next row Switch to Black and knit 2 more rows. Bind off.

FINISHING

Sew the sole and back seams, then sew the sides to the toe. Sew up the top opening for ¼" (0.5cm) starting at the toe.

Using the crochet hook and Black, complete 6 spots by working as follows: ch 4, join with a sl st; fasten off, leaving enough yarn to attach the spot to the bootie. Sew 3 spots onto each side.

Work 4 legs as follows: ch15, turn and beg with 2nd st from hook, work 1 sl st in each st—14 ch sts. Fasten off. Sew a leg back and front at each side of the bootie. Complete a second, identical bootie.

Sweet heather

A pretty posy for Mommy . . .

SOLE

Using Magenta, cast on 38 (40) sts and knit 1 row, then cont in garter st, increasing every 2 rows as follows:

Next row K1, inc 1, k17 (18), inc 1, k2, inc 1, k17 (18), inc 1, k1. Work 1 row straight.

Next row K2, inc 1, k17 (18), inc 1, k4, inc 1, k17 (18), inc 1, k2. Work 1 row straight.

Next row K3, inc 1, k17 (18), inc 1, k6, inc 1, k17 (18), inc 1, k3. Work 1 row straight.

Next row K4, inc 1, k17 (18), inc 1, k8, inc 1, k17 (18), inc 1, k4—54 (56) sts.

Continuing in garter st, work 2 rows Light Green, 2 rows Green.

Next row Switch to Oatmeal and work straight in stockinette st for 6 rows, then dec every 2 rows as follows:

Next row K16 (17), * SKP *, rep from * to * 4

times, k2, ** k2tog **, rep from ** to ** 4 times, k16 (17). Work 1 row straight.

Next row K16 (17), * SKP *, rep from * to * twice, ** k2tog **, rep from ** to ** twice, k16 (17). Work 1 row straight.

Next row K16 (17), SKP, k2, k2tog, k16 (17)—36 (38) sts.

Next row With WS facing, knit to end. Place the first and last 12 sts on stitch holders.

Cont over the central 12 (14) sts in garter st, working 2 rows Green followed by 2 rows Light Green.

Bind off. Using Green, knit across the 12 sts from the first stitch holder, pick up and knit 3 sts along the central band, then cast on 4 (5) sts—19 (20) sts. Knit another row in Green followed by 2 rows Light Green. Bind off.

Complete the other side to match, reversing the shaping as follows: Cast on 4 (5) sts, pick up and knit 3 from the central band, then work across the remaining 12 sts from the holder.

FINISHING

Sew up the sole and back seams. Using the crochet hook and Magenta, make 2 small bobbles. Attach a press stud to each side of the strap, and slip stitch the bobble on the outside.

Make a second bootie to match, reversing the position of the press stud.

For a little ballerina

Pink is my favorite color.

SIZES
*Newborn to 3 months
(3 to 6 months)*

MATERIALS
• *1 1¾oz/50g ball
(approx 174yd/160m)
of Bergère de France
Doussine (wool) in
Chimere (rose)* 🔲
• *size 4 (3.5mm) needles*

STITCHES
garter stitch

GAUGE
*24 sts to 4"/10cm over St
st using size 4 (3.5mm)
needles.
Take time to check
gauge.*

Knit each bootie in a single piece, beginning on one side at the center of the sole and working in the direction of the arrow shown below the diagram.

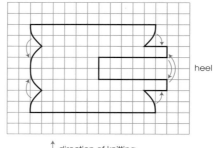

↑ direction of knitting

heel

Cast on 26 (28) sts and knit 1 row then cont in garter st, decreasing every 2 rows as follows: *K1, SK2P, knit until 3 sts remain, k2tog, k1 *. Rep from * to * every 2 rows 4 times—16 (18) sts. Work 1 row straight then shape the heel and toe as follows:

Next row With RS facing, cast on 5 (6) sts, knit until 1 st remains, inc 1, k1. ** Work 1 row straight.

Next row Knit until 1 st remains, inc 1, k1 **. Rep from ** to ** 3 times—26 (29) sts.

Cont straight to end of row 10 then shape upper beg with row 11 as follows:

Next row Bind off 14 (15) sts, then work straight over the remaining 12 (14) sts for 8 rows.

Next row Cast on 14 (15) sts, ** knit until 3 sts remain, k2tog, k1. Work 1 row straight **. Rep from ** to ** 4 times,—16 (18) sts. Now inc for the remaining half-sole as follows:

Next row K1, inc 1, knit until 1 st remains, inc 1, k1. Work 1 row straight. Rep the last 2 rows 4 times—26 (28) sts. Bind off loosely.

BOW
Cast on 20 sts and work in garter st for 4 rows. Bind off. Slipstitch the ends together and flatten the strip with the seam at center back. Wind yarn over the loop a few times in the center to shape the bow; fasten off.

FINISHING
Sew the 2 half-soles together, then sew the heel, the front, and the back of the bootie to the sole. Attach the bow to the opening at center front. Complete a second, identical bootie.

SCARF

SIZE
One size fits all.

MATERIALS
*• 1 1¾oz/50g ball
(approx 164yd/150m)
of Bergère de France
Doussine (wool) in
Chimere (rose)* 🔳
*• size 3 (3.25mm)
needles*

STITCHES
garter stitch

GAUGE
*24 sts and 30 rows to
4"/10cm over St st using
size 4 (3.5mm) needles.
Take time to check
gauge.*

Knit the scarf in a single piece, beginning on one side. Cast on 150 sts and work in garter st for 42 rows. Bind off loosely.

BOW
Cast on 20 sts and work in garter st for 4 rows. Bind off. Slip stitch the ends together and flatten the strip with the seam at center back. Wind yarn over the loop a few times at the center to shape the bow; fasten off.

FINISHING
Complete 4 identical bows and attach 2 at each end of the scarf.

Stripes and bobbles

They're a perfect match for the red dress Mommy bought me . . .

SIZES

*Newborn to 3 months
(3 to 6 months)*

MATERIALS

- *1 1¾oz/50g ball (each
approx 164yd/150m)
each of Cascade 220
Sport (wool) in 2401
Burgundy, 7805 Rose,
7802 Bright Pink, and 9477
Pale Rose* (3)
- *size 5 (3.75mm) needles*
- *size B/1 (2.25mm)
crochet hook*

STITCHES

*garter stitch
striped garter stitch
    2 rows Burgundy
    2 rows Rose
    2 rows Bright Pink
    2 rows Pale Rose
stockinette stitch
k2tog
single dec (SKP)
double dec (SK2P)
crochet bobble*

GAUGE

*24 sts to 4"/10cm over St
st using size 5 (3.75mm)
needles.
Take time to check
gauge.*

SOLE

Using Burgundy, cast on 33 (37) sts and knit 1 row, then cont in striped garter st, increasing every 2 rows as follows:

Next row K1, inc 1, k15 (17), inc 1, k1, inc 1, k15 (17), inc 1, k1. Work 1 row straight.

Next row K2, inc 1, k15 (17), inc 1, k3, inc 1, k15 (17), inc 1, k2. Work 1 row straight.

Next row K3, inc 1, k15 (17), inc 1, k5, inc 1, k15 (17), inc 1, k3. Work 1 row straight.

Next row K4, inc 1, k15 (17), inc 1, k7, inc 1, k15 (17), inc 1, k4. Work 1 row straight.

Next row K5, inc 1, k15 (17), inc 1, k9, inc 1, k15 (17), inc 1, k5—53 (57) sts.

Continuing in striped garter st, work straight for 10 rows and then, beg with next row, dec every 2 rows as follows:

Next row K23 (25), SKP, SK2P, k2tog, k23 (25)—49 (53) sts.

Next row K21 (23), SKP, SK2P, k2tog, k21 (23)—45 (49) sts.

Next row K19 (21), SKP, SK2P, k2tog, k19 (21)—41 (45) sts.

Next row K17 (19), SKP, SK2P, k2tog, k17 (19)—37 (41) sts.

Next row K15 (17), SKP, SK2P, k2tog, k15 (17)—33 (37) sts.

Switch to Pale Rose and knit 2 rows straight, then finish by working in Burgundy for 8 rows. Bind off loosely.

FINISHING

Sew up the sole and back seams. Let the cuff roll naturally. Using the crochet hook make 2 bobbles each in Rose, Bright Pink, and Pale Rose and attach them alternating the colors, to the roll-down cuff. Make a second identical bootie.

Two little mice

Kitty loves to play with my feet.

SIZES
Newborn to 3 months
(3 to 6 months)

MATERIALS
• 1 1¾oz/50g ball
(approx 164yd/150m) of
Rowan Milk Cotton Fine
in #493 Snow (white)
• 1 1¾oz/50g ball (approx
137yd/125m) of Rowan
Purelife Revive in #462
Basalt (dark gray)
• one set (4) size 2
(2.5mm) double-pointed
needles (dpns)
• size B/1 (2.25mm)
crochet hook
• stitch markers

STITCHES
garter stitch
stockinette stitch
single dec (SKP)
crochet chain stitch,
single crochet, slip stitch

GAUGE
30 sts to 4"/10cm over
St st using size 2 (2.5mm)
needles and Milk Cotton
Fine.
Take time to check
gauge.

48

BOOTIE

Beg at the heel: Using size 2 needles and Dark Gray, cast on 8 (10) sts and knit 1 row. Beg with next row, cont in garter st, increasing every 2 rows as follows: * k1, inc 1, knit until 1 st remains, inc 1, k1 **. Work 1 row straight *. Rep from * to * once, then from * to ** once—14 (16) sts. Work 24 (28) rows straight, then beg with next row, dec every 2 rows as follows: * k1, SKP, knit until 3 sts remain, k2tog, k1 **. Work 1 row straight *. Rep from * to * 3 (4) times then from * to ** once—4 sts. Leave on a spare needle.

Using the remaining 2 needles and White, beg at the heel with RS facing, pick up and knit 23 (25) sts on the right side, then the 4 sts from the spare needle followed by 23 (25) sts from the left side—50 (54) sts. Place a stitch marker on each side of the 4 central sts. Using all 4 needles, work in rounds of garter st and form the tip of the muzzle by increasing 1 st on each side of the 4 central sts every 2 rows twice—54 (58) sts.

Next, continuing in garter st, dec 1 st on each side of the 4 central sts (SKP, k4, then k2tog) every 2 rows twice. Then dec 1 st on each side of the 2 central sts every 2 rows 4 times. Finally, dec 1 st on each side of the 4 central sts every 2 rows 4 times—44 (48) sts.
Next row Switch to Dark Gray and work in stockinette st for 4 rows. Bind off loosely.

EARS

Using Dark Gray, cast on 5 sts, knit 1 row, and cont in garter st as follows: K2, inc 1, k1, inc 1, k2. Work 1 row straight.
Next row K3 inc 1, k1, inc 1, k3—9 sts. Work 1 row straight.

Next row ** K1, SKP, k3, k2tog, k1. Work 1 row straight.
Next row K1, SKP, k1, k2tog, k1—5 sts. Work 1 row straight. Bind off. Make a second, identical ear.

WHISKERS

Using the crochet hook and Dark Gray, work 30 ch sts very tightly for the first whisker. Fasten off. Work 25 ch sts very tightly for the second whisker. Fasten off.

TAIL

Using the crochet hook and Dark Gray, work 100 ch sts very tightly for a base chain, turn and, beg with 2nd st on hook, work back with 1 ch st in each of the base chain—99 sts. Fasten off.

MUZZLE

Using the crochet hook and Dark Gray, work 3 ch, 3 sc in the first of the 3 sts just worked, close with a sl st and fasten off.

FINISHING

Sew up the back of the bootie, and attach the tail at center heel, the muzzle at the tip of the nose, and an ear on each side of the center front, as shown in the photo. Use a tapestry needle to embroider the eyes in Dark Gray. Remove the stitch markers. Pass the whiskers under the knit sts at center front and hold them in place with a few little invisible sts, using sewing thread.

Using the crochet hook and Dark Gray, work around the edge of the sole with 1 row of sc over the first row of garter st. Make a second, identical bootie.

High-tops

I'm ready to play in the big leagues!

SIZES

3 to 6 months

(6 to 9 months)

MATERIALS

• *1 1¾oz/50g ball (each approx 164yd/150m) each of Cascade 220 Sport (wool) in 9591 White, 8892 Turquoise, and 9542 Orange*

• *size 5 (3.75mm) needles*

• *size B/1 (2.25mm)*

• *crochet hook*

STITCHES

garter stitch

k2tog

single decrease (SKP)

crochet chain stitch, single crochet, slip stitch, double crochet

GAUGE

24 sts to 4"/10cm over St st using size 5 (3.75mm) needles.

Take time to check gauge.

SOLE

Using the size 5 (3.75mm) needles and White cast on 38 (42) sts. Knit 1 row then cont in garter st and inc every 2 rows as follows:

Next row K2, inc 1, k16 (18) inc 1, k2, inc 1, k16 (18), inc 1, k2. Work 1 row straight.

Next row K3, inc 1, k16 (18), inc 1, k4, inc 1, k16 (18), inc 1, k3. Work 1 row straight.

Next row K4, inc 1, k16 (18), inc 1, k6, inc 1, k16 (18), inc 1, k4. Work 1 row straight.

Next row K5, inc 1, k16 (18), inc 1, k8, inc 1, k16 (18), inc 1, k5. Work 1 row straight.

Next row K6, inc 1, k16 (18), inc 1, k10, inc 1, k16 (18), inc 1, k6—58 (62) sts.

UPPER

Cont in garter st, using 3 colors and loosely twisting the yarn at the back of the work to avoid forming holes when changing colors: K23 (25) Turquoise, k12 White, k23 (25) Orange. Work 10 rows straight as given, then dec on White sts at toe (beg with SKP, end with k2tog) every 2 rows 5 times until 2 White sts remain.

Next row ktog 1 white st with the first Orange st, and ktog the last Turquoise st with the last White st.

Now, for the upper, bind off 13 (15) Orange sts, leave aside the remaining 10 Orange and 10 Turquoise sts for the ankle, bind off the last 13 (15) Turquoise sts. Using White, work across the 20 sts left aside and complete 4 rows in garter st. Bind off loosely. Complete a second high-top bootie, reversing the colors.

FINISHING

Using the crochet hook and White, make 2 circles each in Turquoise and Orange as follows: Work 6 h, join with a sl st in the first ch st, work 3 ch (to count as first dc) followed by 14 dc into loop. Close with a sl st over 3rd ch st at beg; fasten off. Join White yarn with a sl st and work 1 sc over each dc; close with a sl st and fasten off.

Work 160 ch sts very tightly for a lace; fasten off. Repeat for second lace.

Sew up the sole and back seams. Slip stitch the circle to the sides of the heels, reversing the colors.

Thread the lace through each side of the opening to fasten the upper.

Chic stripes

A hat and socks to dress up my onesie.

SIZE
3 to 6 months

MATERIALS
• 1 1¾oz/50g ball (each approx 196yd/180m) each of Bergère de France Caline (acrylic/wool/polyamide) in Carabosse (black) and Nono (gray) (■)
• size 2 (2.75mm) and 3 (3.25mm) needles

STITCHES
stockinette stitch
k2, p2 rib
k2tog, p2tog
single dec (SKP)

GAUGE
26 sts and 36 rows to 4"/10cm over St st using size 3 (3.25mm) needles. Take time to check gauge.

SOCKS

Using size 2 (2.75mm) needles and Black, cast on 30 sts and work in k2, p2 rib until sock measures ¾" (2cm) from cast-on edge. Next row, switch to size 3 (3.25mm) needles and Gray to work in stockinette st for 6 rows, then cont in striped stockinette st as follows: 2 rows Black, 2 rows Gray, 2 rows Black, 6 rows Gray. Beg the half-heel, using black, with RS facing, working in stockinette st over the first 8 sts as follows:

Next row K5, k2tog, k1, turn the work, p7.
Next row K4, k2tog, k1, turn the work, p6.
Next row K3, k2tog, k1, turn the work, p5.
Next row K2, k2tog, k1, turn the work, p4.
Next row K1, k2tog, k1, turn the work, p3.
Next, with RS facing, pick up and knit 1 st every 2 rows 5 times along the knit sts on the edge—8 black sts. The half-heel is complete. Place these 8 sts and the foll 14 sts on a stitch holder or spare needle.
For the second half-heel, using Black, with RS facing, working in stockinette st over the last 8 sts as follows:
Next row K1, SKP, k5, turn the work, p7.
Next row K1, SKP, k4, turn the work, p6.
Next row K1, SKP, k3, turn the work, p5.
Next row K1, SKP, k2, turn the work, p4.
Next row K1, SKP, k1, turn the work, p3.
Next, with RS facing, pick up and knit 1 st every 2 rows 5 times along the knit sts on the edge—8 black sts. The second half-heel is complete. Using Gray, work across all the sts and complete 6 rows in stockinette st, then cont in striped stockinette st as follows: 2 rows Black, 2 rows Gray, 2 rows Black, 6 rows Gray. For the toe, cont in Black and dec every 2 rows as follows:

Next row K6, k2tog, SKP, k10, k2tog, SKP, k6. Work 1 row straight.
Next row K5, k2tog, SKP, k8, k2tog, SKP, k5. Work 1 row straight.
Next row K4, k2tog, SKP, k6, k2tog, SKP, k4. Work 1 row straight.
Next row K3, k2tog, SKP, k4, k2tog, SKP, k3. Work 1 row straight.
Next row K2, k2tog, SKP, k2, k2tog, SKP, k2. Work 1 row straight.
Next row K1, k2tog, SKP, k2tog, SKP, k1—6 sts. Cut the yarn, leaving a length of about 10"(25cm). Pass the yarn through the remaining sts, pull firmly to close and fasten off with a few little sts, then sew up the back seam. Complete a second, identical sock.

HAT

SIZES

*Newborn to 3 months
(3 to 6 months)*

MATERIALS

• *1 1¾oz/50g ball (each
approx 196yd/180m)
each of Bergère de
France Caline (acrylic/
wool/polyamide) in
Carabosse (black) and
Nono (gray)* 🔲

• *size 2 (2.75mm) and 3
(3.25mm) needles*

STITCHES

*stockinette stitch
k2, p2 rib
single dec (SKP)
k2tog/p2tog*

GAUGE

*26 sts and 36 rows
4"/10cm over St st using
size 3 (3.25mm) needles.
Take time to check
gauge.*

Using size 2 (2.75mm) needles and Black, cast on 110 sts and work in k2, p2 rib for ¾" (2cm), beginning and ending even-numbered rows with k2.

Next row Switch to size 3 (3.25mm) needles and Gray, and work in stockinette st , decreasing 12 times evenly across the row—98 sts. Cont in stockinette st for another 5 rows, then switch to striped stockinette st as follows: * 2 rows Black, 2 rows Gray *, rep from * to * 3 times.

Next row Cont in Gray and dec every 2 rows as follows:

Next row K1, * k10, k2tog *, rep from * to * 7 times, k1. Work 1 row straight.

Next row K1, * k9, k2tog *, rep from * to * 7 times, k1. Work 1 row straight.

Next row K1, * k8, k2tog *, rep from * to * 7 times, k1. Work 1 row straight.

Next row K1, * k7, k2tog *, rep from * to * 7 times, k1. Work 1 row straight.

Next row K1, * k6, k2tog *, rep from * to * 7 times, k1. Work 1 row straight.

Next row K1, * k5, k2tog *, rep from * to * 7 times, k1. Work 1 row straight.

Next row K1, * k4, k2tog *, rep from * to * 7 times, k1. Work 1 row straight.

Next row K1, * k3, k2tog *, rep from * to * 7 times, k1. Work 1 row straight.

Switch to Black and cont as follows:

Next row K1, * k2, k2tog *, rep from * to * 7 times, k1. Work 1 row straight.

Next row K1, * k1, k2tog *, rep from * to * 7 times, k1. Work 1 row straight.

Next row K1, * k2tog *, rep from * to * 7 times, k1—10 sts.

Work 6 rows straight in stockinette st. Bind off. Sew up the back seam.

Mushrooms

I'm going with Grandpa to look for mushrooms in the woods.

SIZES

Newborn to 3 months
(3 to 6 months)

MATERIALS

• *1 3oz/100g ball (each approx 220yd/201m) each of Cascade Yarns 220 Superwash (superwash wool) in 801 Green, 907 Orange, 873 Oatmeal, and 910A Cream* (4)
• *size 7 (4.5mm) needles*
• *size B/1 (2.25mm) crochet hook*
• *2 wooden buttons*

STITCHES

garter stitch
stockinette stitch
single dec (SKP)
SK2P
k2tog/p2tog
crochet bobbles, single crochet

GAUGE

20 sts to 4"/10cm over St st using size 7 (4.5mm) needles.
Take time to check gauge.

SOLE

With Green, cast on 32 (36) sts and knit 1 row. Cont in garter st, increasing every 2 rows as follows:
Next row K2, inc 1, k13 (15), inc 1, k2, inc1, k13 (15), inc 1, k2. Work 1 row straight.
Next row K3, inc 1, k13 (15), inc 1, k4, inc1, k13 (15), inc 1, k3. Work 1 row straight.
Next row K4, inc 1, k13 (15), inc 1, k6, inc1, k13 (15), inc 1, k4. Work 1 row straight.
Next row K5, inc 1, k13 (15), inc 1, k8, inc1, k13 (15), inc 1, k5—48 (52) sts.
Cont straight in garter st for 10 rows. Bind off.

MUSHROOM CAP

With Orange, cast on 14 (16) sts and work in garter st for 4 rows. On the next row, switch to stockinette st; cont straight for 7 (9) rows.
Next row K1, SKP, work until 3 sts remain, k2tog, k1. Work 1 row straight.
Next row K1, SKP, SK2P, k2, k2tog, k2tog, k1—6 (8) sts. Bind off.

STEM

Using Oatmeal, cast on 4 sts and work in garter st for 6 rows.
* **Next row** K1, inc 1, knit until 1 st remains, inc 1, k1. Work 1 row straight *. Rep from * to * once—8 sts. Cont straight for 8 rows.
** **Next row** K1, SKP, knit until 3 sts remain, k2tog, k1. Work 1 row straight **. Rep from ** to ** once. Bind off.

BACK BAND

With Green, cast on 3 sts, work in garter st for 10 rows. Bind off loosely.

ANKLE STRAP

With Green, cast on 30 sts and work in garter st for 4 rows. Bind off loosely.

FINISHING

Sew the sole and back seams; fold the back band in half and slip stitch it to the center heel. Sew the mushroom cap to the front of the bootie, then fold the stem in half and slip stitch it to the center underside of the cap. Using Green, work a little loop at one end of the ankle strap and sew the button to the other end. Thread the ankle strap through the back band and the mushroom stem, with the button end nearer the heel to fasten as shown in the photo. Using the crochet hook and Cream, complete 9 bobbles and attach them in staggered rows over the mushroom cap. Using Orange, work 1 row of sc around the edge of the mushroom cap. Complete a second bootie, reversing the position of the ankle strap.

White as snow

Tomorrow we leave for the mountains . . .

SIZES
*Newborn to 3 months
(3 to 6 months)*

MATERIALS
• *1 5oz/140g ball
(approx 362yd/331m) of
Bernat Softee Baby
(acrylic) in 30008
Antique White*
• *2 pairs size 3 (3.25mm)
needles*
• *size B/1 (2.25mm)
crochet hook*

STITCHES
*stockinette stitch
garter stitch
cable stitch (see chart)
pompom
crochet chain stitch*

GAUGE
*26 sts to 4"/10cm over St
st using size 3 (3.25mm)
needles.
Take time to check
gauge.*

SOLE

Beg at the ankle. Cast on 38 sts (both sizes) and work in cable pattern, according to the chart, as follows: * p2, k4 *, rep from * to * 5 times, end with p2. After completing 3 (4) cable cross-overs, leave the first and last 12 sts on spare needles. Use the other needles to work over the central 14 sts, continuing the cable pattern. After completing 6 (8) cross-overs, leave these 14 sts aside and cut the yarn.

With RS facing, work across the first 10 sts left aside, pick up and knit 9 (13) sts along the edge of the sole, then work across the next 10 sts from those left aside—50 (58) sts. Cont in garter st for 10 rows. Now leave the first 19 (23) sts and the last 19 (23) sts on spare needles and cont in garter st over the central 12 sts, working tog the last st of each row with the first st of those left aside until 6 sts remain. Bind off.

FINISHING

Sew up the heel and back seams. Using the crochet hook, work 100 ch sts for a cord. Thread the cord under the cables at the base of the ankle, beg and end at center back. Make 2 little pompoms and attach one to each end of the cord. Tie in a bow. Complete a second, identical bootie.

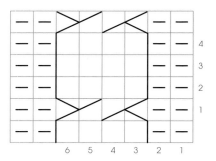

K on RS, p on RS

P on RS, K on RS

4=st RC

Warm and fuzzy

Mommy made these really fast to keep the frost away.

SIZES
Newborn to 3 months
(3 to 6 months)

MATERIALS
• *1 1¾oz/50g ball (each approx 87yd/80m) each of Bergère de France Magic+ (wool acrylic) in Fonte (dark gray) and Silex (light gray)* 🔲
• *1 1¾oz/50g ball (each approx 87yd/80m) each of Bergère de France Teddy (polyamide) in Barbie (rose) and Blanche-Neige(white)* 🔲
• *size 7 (4.5mm) needles*

STITCHES
garter stitch
K2tog
single dec (SKP)

GAUGE
20 sts to 4"/10cm over St st using size 7 (4.5mm) needles and Magic+. Take time to check gauge.

SOLE
Using Gray, cast on 19 (21) sts and knit 1 row, then cont in garter st, increasing every 2 rows as follows:

Next row K1, inc 1, k8 (9), inc 1, k1, inc 1, k8 (9), inc 1, k1. Work 1 row straight.

Next row K2, inc 1, k8 (9), inc 1, k3, inc 1, k8 (9), inc 1, k2. Work 1 row straight.

Next row K3, inc 1, k8 (9), inc 1, k5, inc 1, k8 (9), inc 1, k3. Work 1 row straight.

Next row K4, inc 1, k8 (9), inc 1, k7, inc 1, k8 (9), inc 1, k4—35 (37) sts.

Cont straight in garter st for 6 (8) rows, then dec every 2 rows as follows:

Next row K9 (10), * SKP *, rep from * to * 3 times, k2, ** k2tog **, rep from ** to ** 3 times, k9 (10). Work 3 rows straight.

Next row K7 (8), * SKP *, rep from * to * twice, k1, ** k2tog **, rep from ** to ** twice, k7 (8)—21 (23) sts. Work 3 rows straight.

Next row Switch to Pink or White and cont in garter st for 16 rows. Bind off loosely.

FINISHING
Sew the sole and back seams. Fold over the cuff, leaving the back seam open.

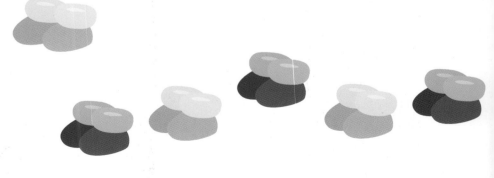

Two bold bears

I've got a big kiss for my teddies . . .

62

SIZES

Newborn to 3 months
(3 to 6 months)

MATERIALS

• *1 1¾oz/50g ball (approx 98yd/90m) of Bergère de France Sport (wool / acrylic) in Campeche (brown)* (A)
• *1 1¾oz/50g ball (each approx 87yd/80m) each of Bergère de France Teddy (polyamide) in Bambie (light brown) and Pantin (beige)* (B)
• *A small amount of black yarn to embroider the eyes and muzzle*
• *size 4 (3.5mm) needles*
• *tapestry needle for embroidery*
• *elastic thread*

STITCHES

garter stitch
k2, p2 rib
knit 2 together
straight stitch
(embroidery)

GAUGE

24 sts to 4"/10cm over St st using size 4 (3.5mm) needles and Sport.
Take time to check gauge.

SOLE

Using Brown yarn, cast on 32 (36) sts and knit 1 row, then cont in garter st, increasing every 2 rows as follows:

Next row K2, inc 1, k13 (15), inc 1, k2, inc 1, k13 (15), inc 1, k2. Work 1 row straight.

Next row K3, inc 1, k13 (15), inc 1, k4, inc 1, k13 (15), inc 1, k3. Work 1 row straight.

Next row K4, inc 1, k13 (15), inc 1, k6, inc 1, k13 (15), inc 1, k4. Work 1 row straight.

Next row K5, inc 1, k13 (15), inc 1, k8, inc 1, k13 (15), inc 1, k5–48 (52) sts.

Cont straight in garter st for 8 rows, then shape the upper as follows: K28 (30), k2tog, turn the work, k9, k2tog, turn the work. Continue over the central 9 sts, working tog the last st of each row with the first st of those left aside, until 30 (34) sts remain. Now, knit to end of row, and knit 1 row. Next, using Brown bouclé yarn, cont in k2, p2 rib for 2" (5cm). Finish off by working 2 more rows in k2, p2 rib using either the Light Brown or Beige bouclé yarn.

MUZZLE

Using either the Light Brown or the Beige bouclé yarn, cast on 6 sts and knit 1 row. *Next row K1, inc 1, knit until 1 st remains, inc 1, k1. Work 1 row straight *. Rep from * to * once more. Knit straight for 4 rows then dec as follows: ** k1, SKP, knit until 3 sts remain, k2tog, k1. Work 1 row straight **. Rep from ** to ** once more. Bind off.

EARS

Using either the Light Brown or the Beige bouclé yarn, cast on 8 sts, knit 4 rows, then dec as follows: *K1, SKP, knit until 3 sts remain, k2tog, k1. Work 1 row straight *. Rep from * to * once more. Bind off. Complete a second, identical ear.

FINISHING

Using Black, embroider the nose and mouth over the muzzle, as shown in the photo. Using the crochet hook and Black, make 2 eyes as follows: Work 3 ch sts, then * yo, insert hook into first of the 3 sts just worked, yo and through first 2 lps on hook *, rep from * to * twice, then yo and through all lps on hook. Sew the sole and back seams, then slip stitch the muzzle to the toe, the eyes just above the muzzle, and an ear to each side of the bootie. Pass the elastic thread through the first row of ribbing.

Make a matching bootie, changing the color of the bouclé yarn.

Index

Standard Yarn Weight System

Yarn Weight Symbol & Category Names	0 Lace	1 Super Fine	2 Fine	3 Light	4 Medium	5 Bulky	6 Super Bulky
Type of Yarns in Category	Fingering 10 count crochet thread	Sock, Fingering, Baby	Sport, Baby	DK, Light Worsted	Worsted, Afghan, Aran	Chunky, Craft, Rug	Bulky, Roving
Knit Gauge Range* in Stockinette Stitch to 4 inches	33 –40** sts	27–32 sts	23–26 sts	21–24 sts	16–20 sts	12–15 sts	6–11 sts
Recommended Needle in Metric Size Range	1.5–2.25 mm	2.25–3.25 mm	3.25–3.75 mm	3.75–4.5 mm	4.5–5.5 mm	5.5–8 mm	8 mm and larger
Recommended Needle U.S. Size Range	000 to 1	1 to 3	3 to 5	5 to 7	7 to 9	9 to 11	11 and larger
Crochet Gauge* Ranges in Single Crochet to 4 inch	32-42 double crochets**	21–32 sts	16–20 sts	12–17 sts	11–14 sts	8–11 sts	5–9 sts
Recommended Hook in Metric Size Range	Steel*** 1.6–1.4mm Regular hook 2.25 mm	2.25–3.5 mm	3.5–4.5 mm	4.5–5.5 mm	5.5–6.5 mm	6.5–9 mm	9 mm and larger
Recommended Hook U.S. Size Range	Steel*** 6, 7, 8 Regular hook B–1	B–1 to E–4	E–4 to 7	7 to I–9	I–9 to K–10½	K–10½ to M–13	M–13 and larger

Categories of yarn, gauge ranges, and recommended needle and hook sizes

* GUIDELINES ONLY: The above reflect the most commonly used gauges and needle or hook sizes for specific yarn categories.

** Lace weight yarns are usually knitted or crocheted on larger needles and hooks to create lacy, openwork patterns. Accordingly, a gauge range is difficult to determine. Always follow the gauge stated in your pattern.

*** Steel crochet hooks are sized differently from regular hooks--the higher the number, the smaller the hook, which is the reverse of regular hook sizing.

This Standards & Guidelines booklet and downloadable symbol artwork are available at: YarnStandards.com